MEDIA THAT TRANSFORMS NATIONS

Capturing Life, Communicating Hope

By Calvin & Carol Conkey

MEDIA - IT'S EVERYWHERE!

S mall roadside fires lit our way as we walked dusty cobblestone lanes in the foothills of India's Himalayas, late one cold winter night. We passed villagers squatting around steamy pots of rice and lentils, women selling meals to local passersby, and others warming their hands near the open flames while discussing the days' events. Flashing lights in the distance caught our eye, so we followed the path past several yaks tied to a post. Entering a dingy room, we saw an unlikely sight: several Tibetan youth crowded over video arcade games. The next shop held floor-to-ceiling videos, including "Back to the Future 2" -- which at that time, had not yet been released to theaters in America! Media had captured the attention of these remote, unreached people.

Crafting the Message

Since we started the media ministry Create International in 1989, the many documented accounts we've received have convinced us of the essential role of media in discipling the nations. From the interest stirred by new technologies like Ipods to the heart response to a message communicated through traditional art forms, the Spirit-led use of media to impact individuals and nations is an enormous factor in our effectiveness to fulfill Jesus' mandate to disciple the nations. The acid test of effective media is not how nice it looks, nor how many compliments are given; the proof is in seeing souls enter the Kingdom of God and communities transformed.

Komering of Indonesia

Not long ago, a short-term ministry team nervously stepped into the small home of a Muslim family in the highly restricted area of South Sumatra, Indonesia. The two team members sat on the only stools available as the others gathered around on the dirt floor. Through an interpreter they explained that they had come to show a new video in the Komering language. The family smiled approval and removed a lace cloth to reveal a large television set! As the visitors silently prayed that their video would be a powerful testimony, the family's excitement grew with the anticipation of seeing a video in their own language for the first time.

The father watched skeptically as the culturally-adapted video of the "Prodigal Son" began, but he kept inching closer to the screen as the story unfolded. As the truths of Christ's sacrifice and the great love of God were explained in their own heart-language, everyone in the room watched intently. At the end of the showing, the father's nose was nearly touching the screen as he exclaimed excitedly, "This is the very first movie I have ever seen in my own language and I like it very much. Everything in it is true. It is very good!"

In response to the family's open hearts, the team provided follow-up through long-term missionaries and, as a result, home fellowships were formed to study the life of Jesus. There is now an indigenous Komering church in Sumatra—the least evangelized island in the world.

◆ ◆ ◆

COMMUNICATION TO ALL PEOPLES

W hen we think of utilizing new technologies for furthering the Kingdom of God in all the nations, it is vital to present the message in a way that is both understandable and relevant to the culture of the people.

Consider the implications: over four billion people — about two thirds of the world's population -- are oral learners. Orality refers to the implications of how people think, learn, remember and communicate because of their reliance on orally expressed stories, narratives, songs and proverbs. They do not convey or receive information through written means such as books or tracts, or any form of communication that utilizes linear thinking. Included in this group are those who may read a written language, but it is not the way they prefer to interact with the world -- and the Word of God. Surprisingly, the latter group includes millions of young men and women, a generation called "postmodernists" who live in "literate societies" but prefer nonliterate means of communication such as television and internet. With today's technology, many non-literate peoples are moving directly into visual and oral means of learning and communication without ever learning to read and write their own heart language.

If these oral learners are to truly "hear" the gospel of Christ (understand, internalize, and recall the message), it must come to them through proverbs, prose, or carefully constructed stories compatible with their cultural thinking and presentation style.

We must contextualize our message to the worldview of those we seek to reach. Jesus modeled how to impart truth in culturally relevant ways; we can learn from Him how to discover, interpret, and employ redemptive analogies (the witness which He has left for Himself).[1] This ability was also displayed in an Athenian cultural context by one of the New Testament's most effective cross-cultural missionaries, the Apostle Paul: "Now what you worship as something unknown I am going to proclaim to you" (Acts 17:23).

East Java, Indonesia

A tiny Indonesian village house soon filled with cigarette smoke from the men who had gathered to play a part in our drama. Only recently had their language been put in written form. One of the actors could not read at all and others were struggling to make sense of the translated lines. In the middle of casting, a distinguished looking Islamic leader entered the room. Our hearts raced as he scolded us, "You can't do this drama here!" We innocently inquired, "Why not?" He scoffingly replied, "These are a bunch of uneducated fools. You will never be able to do any sort of worthwhile drama with them." He then stormed out of the room. Sighing with relief, we remembered God's Word: "But God chose the foolish things of the world to shame the wise" (1 Cor. 1:27).

During the filming, the Muslim participants would stop and pray or go off to the local mosque whenever they heard their call to prayer. Our Create crew decided to use this time in like manner. The actors would watch us, sometimes mock us, but we knew the truths of the script and scriptures they were dramatizing were affecting them. We fervently interceded that they would become followers of Isa al Masih-Jesus the anointed Savior.

A few months after our return to Australia, a missionary from that people group came to report to us, "Your evangelistic film is working me out of a job!" He went on to explain: after our departure, the whole cast of seven became believers through further discipleship with our Indonesian cultural advisor! They formed home groups and had already distributed a hundred copies of the evangelistic video to their friends and family. Many workers have reported that this dramatic film is very relevant to the culture and has gained wide acceptance amongst this large unreached people group of East Java. Because this film is produced in the local language, it is now on the top of the charts in the area video rentals and sales.

THE VISION

Stories like these point to the fruitfulness of developing contextualized media tools for unreached peoples. The vision for nation discipling is to see men and women reconciled to God, released into their gifting and finding their place in fulfilling the Great Commission. They will do so as they are free to worship and work through their cultural expressions, in order to impact their people group to see transformation in every sphere of their shared life.

"As we pursue the task of world evangelization, we must identify the major priorities that will be integral to ensuring that all the peoples of the world will have the opportunity to hear the gospel, in their "heart" language, near where they live, with access to a healthy, indigenous church to help them grow in faith."[2]

The Strategy

How do we get there? There are keys to discovering the most strategic way to bring heart understanding and transformation to a people group. We must understand the needs, the most effective media to use, and the cultural context for the message in order to create a strategy, message and tool that are unique for each people.

In our dramatic film stories, we show people coming to crisis through a real, current issue in their culture, and then being exposed to Christ as the answer. They may meet a believer, have a dream, or find scriptures that speak to their problem. There's often an invitation given within the context of the story, actually showing the main character coming to Christ, then sharing their new faith with family and friends, and entering into fellowship. This is a key to the evangelism, as community oriented cultures shy away from individual conversion as it can mean complete isolation. Seeing families open to the gospel and believers from their own culture in contextualized fellowship is very reassuring and gives them the courage to step out, regardless of the response of those immediately around them.

The stories continue, showing the outworking of the character's new faith to address the crisis, and then being an influence on those around them. In this way we're able to sow the seed that personal transformation should lead to social transformation (Matt. 28:18). Until the Church exists in a people group, Kingdom transformation of the spheres of that society cannot occur.

Banjara People of India

Filming in the Banjara village in central India gave us the opportunity to become living witnesses for Jesus. Our team was often asked to pray for people in their homes. Only a few families in this village were Christian, so it was not uncommon to be praying beneath photos or shrines of Hindu gods. As Hindu/animists, the Banjara look to the supernatural to demonstrate the reality of one's faith in God. Less than 1% of over 20 million Banjara were believers.

Our team scripted and produced a film that spoke into a critical issue for the Banjara: community conflict. Many lives were lost from the cycle of retribution and vengeance the Banjara were caught up in. Our film, entitled "Transformation," did just that in the Banjara community. As the only film in the Banjara language, they were im-

mediately drawn in as they saw their culture and language honored. National leaders have reported that this film is an historic event in effective outreach to the Banjara people and that tens of thousands of Banjara have given their life to the Lord. We're seeing transformation take hold as well: drunken men have turned from alcohol and are rebuilding their lives and families; home fellowships have started. National workers are requesting more copies, projectors and greater distribution throughout India to further spread the gospel amongst the nomadic Banjara.

A critical stage in the process for an individual or a people group is moving from salvation into growing as a Christian. As we wrestled with the needs of these new believers, God led us to use the same principles we had in creating evangelistic films to develop a DVD depicting a Turkish home fellowship in a Turkish home, with believers dressed in local clothing and speaking Turkish.

The Turks of Turkey

After creating the DVD highlighting the home fellowship group, we were filming an evangelistic drama for the Turks, and we noticed several of the actors excitedly reading a major Turkish magazine. To our surprise, we saw shots of our home fellowship film as illustrations for one of the feature articles in this nationwide magazine. The actors translated the articles for us; it was describing the recent home church movement in Turkey in a positive manner! We were a little nervous that this massive publicity might deter the Turkish believers' participation in this present film. Instead, one of them declared, "It is positive, the media is doing the job for us!" Because our film was very Turkish and adapted to the culture, the local media and Muslim leaders were open to receive the presentation into their society.

THE PROCESS

I n creating any new communication piece, the process begins with an invitation from field workers and nationals to insure that the media tools will be used and there is a distribution plan for ongoing usage. Much time is spent prayerfully hearing God's direction and advice for what media tools to develop as well as the overall message to reach the intended people group.

Creating communication pieces is a partnership between the Holy Spirit and us. As we do the research, we are continually in prayer asking the Lord to give us revelation about the people and the keys to reaching them. We find He says to us: "Come join Me in what I'm already doing among this people." We need to do our best to be skilled workman to know how to best communicate to a people. And when we pray, God will highlight what's key for that time for that group from the research we've done.

It's important to do extensive research before all projects. There is usually at least three months of research and gaining knowledge from field missionaries about effective communication, i.e. what has worked, what hasn't, how the people communicate and share knowledge with each other, what are their felt needs, what hinders them from being a follower of Christ, etc.

Every script is tailor made for the specific audience. In the scripting process, our team addresses community issues such as revenge killings, unforgiveness, superstition, ancestor worship, stealing, etc. The salvation message is interwoven in a drama of conflict and resolution. Local cultural advisors are key to the film's authenticity. We look for a local person, preferably but not necessarily a believer, who's not highly westernized, and has a great love for their culture. If we're able to find more than one, we look for a range of ages, from both sexes, and from various walks of life to get the widest perspective possible.

Key questions to identify the message:
- Gather information from libraries, the Internet, people profiles and outreach experiences,
- Look for reoccurring themes and patterns,
- Study cultural stories, sayings, legends and life stories,
- Analyze the social needs and problems among the people (felt needs or longings)
- Look for redemptive ideas, gospel bridges or themes, morals,
- Discover what the people strive for in life - what do they want to be or accomplish
- Build on biblical truth, biblical values and biblical themes found in the culture

Key questions to identify the method/media:
- What is everyday life like for this people group? Occupations, living conditions, educational levels, literacy and use of technology,
- What are some of their unique and cherished art forms?
- What kind of media is most popular? What do they use to communicate with each other?
- How do the people celebrate ritual events, especially religious ones
- Begin to create a believable story and test it's validity with cultural advisors
- Identify the key person of influence in the culture and portray them as the role models for communicating the gospel.

During production, we regularly ask for input from our cultural advisors to determine the best usage of symbols and other cultural preferences, appropriate gestures and body language, realistic costuming, props, settings, and appropriate emotional expression. After editing the presentation, we field test it for linguistic and cultural accuracy. Once the presentation is being used on the field, we stay in touch with those who are using it to evaluate our effectiveness--did the audience understand the message of the film? How did they respond? How can other media help their growth in coming to faith in Christ and being discipled in God's ways?

SELECTING THE MEDIA

After selecting a message, the next set of questions is selecting the media which will have the greatest impact. Options range from the "wow" of new technology to the comfort and authority of familiar art forms. It's also vital to seek God for how to effectively put together different media for different parts of the process from salvation to discipleship to community transformation.

We must package the Good News in a way that our target people group can unwrap in order to hear with understanding and pass it on with accuracy. Until we learn to share information as local people do, we will have little impact on their community. Let's look at a few media forms as tools of communication which are effective for reaching oral peoples, including this current generation:

Today's Technology

Films are a powerful medium that attracts a wide audience of viewers. Watching a film is a community activity, therefore it is an effective means for a group of people to be exposed to the same message at the same time. It's a powerful way to get the message across because everyone loves dramatic stories. Jesus knew this, and that's one reason why He spoke in parables.

"Dollar for dollar more people come to the Lord through films than any other way. It's inexpensive if it's done right."[3]

One example of an effective use of film is the "Jesus Film." Campus Crusade for Christ reports that the film has been translated into more than 1,000 "heart languages" of the unreached peoples with estimates of 6.1 billion "exposures" and over 200 million conversions.[4] Many agencies and churches have partnered together to distribute millions of their films in video compact disc (VCD) and DVD formats worldwide. More recently the Internet has leveled the playing field, and made it possible for even small ministries to reach millions with their films and animation online.

Radio

Shortwave radio has been used widely to propagate the gospel all over the world for many years. There's been a tremendous response to broadcasts, and many people who would otherwise not have access to the Word of God have received it in their own language through this technology. However, fewer and fewer commonly used radios are being manufactured with the ability to receive the shortwave frequencies, shrinking the audience of major radio ministries each year. Most of these ministries are shifting their focus to more attractive communication technologies like the Internet, where podcasting is rapidly becoming the new tool of choice. Streaming audio and video is becoming commonplace, while those who can afford it are moving to high quality satellite radio broadcast.

Internet

The continuing growth of the internet is phenomenal. In many countries, internet usage is doubling every 100 days![5] Internet usage is increasing in several Middle Eastern countries by more than 200%.[6] Most students worldwide have free access to the internet; among graduates and young professionals, internet access in many countries may be as high as 90%. Even in impoverished countries citizens have access through their schools, government offices and businesses. Internet cafes are popping up all over the unevangelized world and are particularly popular in poorer countries where "pay-for-use" phone shops are very common. This is strategically significant information for those wanting to influence the new generation of unreached peoples and nations. The challenge to the church is to use the internet for evangelism! "The internet is the first medium that allows anyone with reasonably inexpensive equipment to publish to a wide audience. It is the first medium that distributes information globally at almost no cost."[7]

Mobile phones

The "high-touch high-tech" nature of mobile phones has sparked a revolution in communications in developing nations around the world. Many so called "high touch" cultures that are highly relational are attracted to technologies that will improve their feeling of connectedness. Turn off these people's electricity for a day or so and there is little complaint, but take away their mobile phones for 5 minutes and you'll have a riot on your hands! With the advent of high-speed internet capable mobile phones, much of the two-thirds world will bypass the need for computers to access the internet's vast resources.

Microchip Players

Solar powered microchip players provide audio Bible stories with no need for electricity, and are only the size of a credit card. Christian organizations are using these audio players to bring God's message of hope and love to non-reading people all over the world. From evangelism to pastoral training, these solid-state Mega Voice audio players from Galtronix can be programmed in any language.[8]

Wireless Technology

Wireless technology is another development which is rapidly revolutionizing the way we access the internet. There are now a plethora of technologies such as Bluetooth and WIFI which connect computers with mobile phones, PDAs, (personal digital assistant), printers, digital cameras, refrigerators, and every other type of electrical appliance. This has been called the beginning of the second wireless revolution.

Satellite Linkage

The use of satellite in the propagation of the gospel goes far beyond just TV, but also to radio, cellular communications systems, the internet and more. We can be in touch with people thousands of miles away in an instant. Even in some of the least developed nations satellite dishes are surprisingly prevalent.

Communication technology is reshaping the world around us. Previously, to communicate with tens of thousands or even millions of people in their own language, one needed to utilize very expensive high tech electronic media. Now, with the ability to capture the message using new digital technology combined with careful cultural research, reaching the masses cheaply and effectively is possible!

Cultural Arts

Serious consideration must be given to the non-technical media already available in the audience's culture. The Christian message conveyed through a familiar indigenous expression is far more likely to be embraced by the audience than the same message introduced through a strange or foreign media.

New Christians who have received the message through a familiar media can quickly pass the message on to others, without needing to spend time learning a foreign media. Traditional cultural forms such as music, art, storytelling, and dance can be redirected to reveal one's true relationship with God and to communicate His message of love and salvation.

Tibetan Buddhists

Tibetans, for example, portray their Buddhist teachings in a circular type of artwork called a "thangka" painting. A missionary working among the Tibetans in Nepal gave the gospel of Luke to a professional thangka painter, and asked him to paint what he read. What he painted was truly amazing! In the typical circular format, this thangka depicts the life of Christ with meticulous clarity showing the birth, miracles, teachings, last supper, death on the cross, burial, resurrection and ascension. The artist clearly presented how Jesus, coming from the outside, broke through the futility of the "Karma chain" by his resurrection.

We utilized this local media in one of our evangelistic films created to reach Tibetan Buddhists. After viewing it, Tibetans say things like: "Jesus can really liberate me?" "There are other Tibetans that believe in Jesus?" "How can I become a believer in this Jesus?"[9] To add to the excitement, the painter of the thangka became a Christian and is walking with the Lord today.[10]

The Tibetan case study illustrates an important principle: to be effective communicators, we must not only translate what we want to say into the appropriate language, but also communicate our message using the appropriate cultural symbols so that our audience is able to readily understand.

Contextual media is also the best form to insure continued use by the audience. We learned this during a project in West Sumatra, where our team was filming a dramatic rendition of the "Prodigal Son" parable.

Minang, West Sumatra
One of our actors was Muslim, and by the end of the filming he gave his life to the Lord. Part of what impressed him was that our team cared enough to make a film adapted to his Minang culture. When this actor, a prominent singer and entertainer in the Minang culture, proudly showed us some of his music cassettes, we challenged him to now produce and sing music for his culture that would glorify the

Lord. For the next few years, we prayed for him and challenged any team going to Sumatra to visit him and encourage him in producing music that would help bring people to the Lord.

Two years later, a team from Singapore was visiting that same area in Sumatra and heard of a local dance and music performance. They all attended and were overjoyed to hear the gospel woven into the presentation in a way that was non-offensive to the majority Muslim audience, and was very professionally done. After the show they talked with the manager of this dance troupe and found out he was the former actor from our film! He shared that our team had challenged him and showed him how to use the arts to present the gospel. He continues to rise to the challenge, winning people to Jesus using Minang cultural art forms.

We are continually discovering ways in which we can best use the indigenous arts of a culture to convey the gospel message-- but so much more could be done in this area. Christian workers around the world should be paying special attention to how this can be encouraged and promoted in their work, especially among unreached peoples.

AN INTEGRATED MEDIA STRATEGY

Since no single medium can do the whole job effectively, focus-groups and other research methods should be employed to establish which media work best for each stage of the discipling process. It would be worthwhile to survey both non-believers and new believers with the following questions:

--Which media attracted you to know about Jesus?

--Which media was most effective in communicating the gospel message to you?

--Which media helped you grow in your faith?

Missions' current need is not for a new, one-time approach, but for a coordinated process that combines various media forms over a period of time.[11] The combined use of multi-media elements, e.g. music and visuals, increases the emotive and persuasive appeal of the presentation. It's also key to remember that media alone is not enough; "media combined with human interaction is one of the most effective means of communication."[12] A follow-up with group discussion also increases retention and allows for clarification of the message.

Media can optimize every level of church growth and discipling nations. For instance:

- Radio spots and flyer distribution could spark community interest in attending a movie or short video showing.
- At the movie showing, tracts or audio cassettes could be distributed. Having a printed tract or audio tool in hand for people can help bring the message home to them as individuals, giving them something to take home and reflect on privately.
- The distributed literature or verbal request could extend an invitation to a home Bible study; Christians in the Bible study then develop relationships that lead to a conversion of the attendee.
- After conversion, a workbook and video for new Christians could be used to enhance the Bible study during the week; radio and TV programs could help the new believer grow in faith.
- A multimedia kit (DVDs, workbook and correspondence) could be given to the new leaders providing discipleship in some aspect of Biblical education, or perhaps an internet Bible training course, including streaming video of lecturers and graphic illustrations of the lessons.
- A short film might be helpful to depict a home group studying the Bible, but a group of believers might find it helpful to also have a workbook for their times of Bible study so each can prepare beforehand and record their own thoughts and prayers.)
- A new church could learn evangelism and cross-cultural ministry through video profiles, prayer booklets to go out to minister to another unreached people group.

The 6500 distinct unreached people groups of the world[13] reflect the incredible complexity, diversity and greatness of our God. One media form, or one message, will not reach them all. Several mission organizations get some help with the necessary research and planning of the effective use of media through media strategists. These strategists can help missionaries consider how to effectively use media in five different tactical areas: evangelism, conversion, discipleship, leadership training, church planting, and initiating church planting movements.

Calvin and Carol Conkey

EVANGELISM TO CHURCH PLANTING

Discipling New Believers

Discipleship tools are being created to help new believers understand how they could start contextual home fellowships that are both faithful to Scripture and relevant to their culture. The response to these videos has been dramatic. The local actors, themselves believers from a Muslim background, told us that these films would also be very effective for evangelism. Testimony after testimony of people who have given their lives to the Lord after viewing these presentations have emphasized this truth.

In South Sumatra, a new believer was viewing the contextual worship video with his wife who was not yet a believer. After the presentation, his wife exclaimed, "If that is what you have been talking about, then yes I am interested, I could worship Jesus like that!" One of the participants in the film, an actual church planting leader in the community, showed the Indonesian contextual gathering film to the Islamic evangelistic association in his area. After viewing the film, one of the Muslim leaders said "I believe in Isa al Mashi (Jesus the anointed Saviour) how can I become a believer and be baptized?

One of the greatest hindrances for Muslims to come to Christ is their preconceived idea about the nature and practice of Christians. If they can see that there are Followers of Jesus who look like and worship like they do, they see how they too could be a part of this new family—a family who love and follow the teachings of Jesus (Isa in Arabic) and who also remain "fully submitted to God" (which is the call of all Muslims). God knew that this type of presentation was just what many Muslims were waiting to see and hear. Contextual worship videos are available for Indonesians, Algerians, Kurds, Turks, Urdus, Hindis and Thai peoples.

Urdu Speakers of India

"Yes, we're using the same Create International teaching CD on contextual worship. We used to just plant one fellowship every week. But now, every day we go to a different house and tell them to invite their friends and family to come in and we're starting a new Jamat (contextual house church) every day in our area." This exciting report was told to me while on a recent trip to India.

National church planting leaders have seen a tremendous break-through among the Urdu speaking Muslims of India. Reports indicate they have recently baptized 750 new believers and around 7,000 are waiting to receive baptism. They have started 180 Jamats (contextual house churches) in one area and 120 in another area, which already had 2,000 baptized believers.[14] It was incredible to hear of real break-through among the peoples of Northern India.

God is actively working in each people group and invites our participation with Him. He is revealing Himself through dreams and visions, miraculous healings and other manifest-ations of the Spirit's power. As workers we need to also be involved in bold and abundant proclamation of the Word, dem-onstrations of love, humble service, transformed lives and relationship. It is these realities that bring many people to Christ—and we rejoice with this fruit that we are seeing. Greater contextualization of the gospel message will lead to lasting fruit as the community embraces the message within their cultural context.

PUTTING IT ALL TOGETHER

At this point in history, while we carefully select the most effective technologies for each context, there is an even larger movement towards integrating the technologies themselves. The "convergence" of television, satellite, mobile telecommunications, and the internet will spark a revolution in how we see and interact with our world. It will literally launch the world into an unprecedented free-flow of information that will dwarf the effect experienced by the invention of the printing press!

Almost overnight, the simplest evangelistic websites will have an international television ministry. Those who have a presence on the internet now, will be first in line to reap the rewards. All of this has brought the Internet closer than ever before to over a billion people. As Christians we stand at a very important point in human history and the evangelization of the world. We must be prepared to take advantage of this exciting new innovation.

Hindus of India

India. In a land of one billion, mostly without Christ, the Gospel's progress needs to be accelerated—instead of hindered. The family and social community of the 700 million Hindus of this nation will provide a natural relationship for worship and church gathering. Working in partnership with several mission agencies, Create International has produced a culturally adopted evangelistic film in the Hindi language, as well as a follow-up discipleship film that demonstrates how to start contextual home fellowships. Along with these two media tools we have also created a Hindu evangelistic website which contains further contextual evangelistic and discipleship materials.

These three communication technology tools are interwoven together as a holistic transformational media package. When the evangelistic film is viewed it gives links to the discipleship materials which include the contextual home fellowship training video and the website which is in Hindi and English. When the website is accessed, both of the video tools are available for viewing as streaming media, as well as downloadable for duplication and distribution.

Because of the popularity and low cost of VCD technology in India, thousands of copies of these two films have been distributed all over the country. In addition, millions of households are able to view it as several Christian TV ministries are showing the film. These ministries are doing follow-up response with their viewers and referring them to the website and other discipleship materials available in their heart languages. Field missionaries and national workers report that Hindu people are contacting them for more information after viewing the film or website.

CALL TO ACTION

Passion and determination are two keys to being an effective communicator: passion for the Lord and His heart to reach all peoples, and determination to keep pressing-on despite obstacles. We must never give up until all peoples have heard! Media production can be relatively expensive and time consuming, but when the goal is clear, the creativity, energy and resourcefulness are released to get the job done effectively! As communicators of the good news, we must constantly be seeking to utilize all forms of technology to ensure wider and more efficient communication of our message worldwide. Communicators must work hard to choose the appropriate media to communicate a contextualized message for salvation, discipleship, and community transformation.

All the passion and determination in the world still falls short unless our ministries are anointed, and only humility will generate the blessing of God. He wants our involvement, using all of our gifts, by all possible means, to bring all the nations the greatest story ever told. Let's take full advantage of all the multiplicity of media forms, ask God for new insight and creativity, and together with Him create new communication tools that will bring salvation and transformation to the unreached.

God has millions of new ways to reach the peoples of this Earth, and he will give them to us if we seek him earnestly. The

Apostle Paul's words ring true for us today, *"...*so that *by all possible means* I might save some"* (1 Cor. 9: 22).

Have We Exhausted All Possible Means?

In discipling all peoples, and finishing the task of world evangelization, we must follow the admonitions of the Apostle Paul, "It has always been my ambition to preach the gospel where Christ was not known, so that I would not be building on someone else's foundation. Rather, as it is written: 'Those who were not told about him will see, and those who have not heard will understand'" (Rom. 15:20, 21). Paul's ambition and devotion to God's call to extend the Kingdom of God, ignited a passion in him that could not be quenched. A passion that drove him to the frontiers.

Following his example, let's take the gospel to *all* peoples, discipling *all* nations.

◆ ◆ ◆

For more information and resources see
www.createinternational.com and www.indigitube.tv

Bibliography

Barrett, David. *Our Globe and How To Reach It.* Birmingham, AL: New Hope, 1990.

Engel, James. *How Can I Get Them to Listen?* Grand Rapids: Zondervan Publishing House, 1977.

Hesselgrave, David. *Communicating Christ Cross-culturally.* Grand Rapids: Zondervan, 1978.

Hiebert, Paul. *Cultural Anthropology.* Grand Rapids: Baker Book House, 1976.

Hiebert, Paul. *Anthropological Insights for Missionaries.* Grand Rapids: Baker Book House, 1985.

Klem, Herbert. *Oral Communication of Scripture.* Pasadena: William Carey Library, 1982.

McLuhan, Marshall. *Understanding Media: The Extensions of Man.* New York: McGaw-Hill, 1966.

Miles Smith-Morris, ed. *The Economist Book of Vital World Statistics.* New York: Economist Books Ltd., 1990.

Nicholls, Kathleen. *Asian Arts and Christian Hope.* New Delhi: Select Books, 1983.

Nida, Eugene. *Customs and Culture.* New York: Harper and Row, 1954 (Reprinted Pasadena CA: William Carey Library 1975).

Nida, Eugene. *Message and Mission: The Communication of the Christian Faith.* NY: Harper and Brothers, 1960.

Richardson, Don. *Eternity in their Hearts.* California: Regal Books, 1984.

Roper, Don. *"What is Group Media?"* WACC Journal. London: World Association of Christian Communication, 1983.

Shaw, Daniel. *Transculturation.* Pasadena: William Carey Library, 1988.

Soggard, Viggo. *Applying Christian Communication.* Ann Arbor, MI: University Microfilms, 1986.

Soggard, Viggo. *Media in Church and Mission.* Pasadena, CA: William Carey Library, 1993.

Tsering, Marku. *Sharing Christ in the Tibetan Buddhist World.* Upper Darby: Tibet Press, 1988.

---

[1] See Don Richardson'S *Eternity in Their Hearts* for wonderful stories of discovering the truths already in the culture which point to God and His ways.

[2] Paul Eshleman, Lausanne Congress on Evangelism Strategy Chairman in remarks made to "Lausanne Younger Leaders Gathering," Kuala Lumpur, Malaysia, Sept. 2006. http://www.lausanne.org/Brix?pageID=19954.

[3] Mark Snowden, IMB Media strategist, 2000 media conference [www.new-Way.org (accessed 2000)].

[4] "About Us," in *The Jesus Film Project,* A Ministry of Campus Crusade for Christ, International, http://www.jesusfilm.org/aboutus/index.html (accessed April 2007).

[5] Tony Whittaker, *Bulletin of Web Evangelism,* http://guide.gospelcom.net/resources/bulletin.php. Web-Evangelism Guide, SOON Ministries (accessed 2000).

[6] http:// www.internetworldstats.com (accessed April 2007).

[7] Tony Whittaker, *Bulletin of Web Evangelism,* http://guide.gospelcom.net/resources/bulletin.php. Web-Evangelism Guide, SOON Ministries (accessed 2000).

[8] http:///megavoice.com.

[9] Tibetan worker's personal communication, letter in 1992.

[10] Report from field missionaries in Tibet, 2000.

[11] Viggo Sogaard, *Everything You Need to Know for a Cassette Ministry* (Minneapolis: Bethany House, 1975), 34.

[12] Don Roper, "What is Group Media?," *World Association for Christian Communications Journal* (1983).

[13] www.joshuaproject.net

[14] Report from Paul Eshleman, Strategy Leader for "Finishing the Task", Quoted in *Update* 2007, an email communication of Create International. For other reports and streaming evangelistic videos in a variety of languages and cultural settings, see https://www.createinternational.com.

www.ingramcontent.com/pod-product-compliance
Lightning Source LLC
Chambersburg PA
CBHW050354290526
45785CB00006B/2771